Thoug

Soul

With love and great vibes

Cashmere

ISBN-13: 978-0692582091
ISBN-10: 0692582096

Dedication

To the Harper-Bell Family,
Kailyn Saraah Broadway, Samantha Jo Dato

Table of Contents

Introduction

It's like nowadays you have to be a victim of something to be heard. You have to have this juicy story of overcoming some horrific trauma to be news worthy. They want use to reenact, and relive the violence we have lived. Or you have to video an act of violence or put on a wig and use profanity to be seen.

Hard work means nothing unless you are working hard with a missing limb or have started from a state of poverty or homelessness. You are either under qualified or over qualified. There is no room in the world for the "average" hard worker. You are a "nobody" in a place where there's so much pressure to be somebody.

"You are a nobody"... That is a statement only a lost soul believes. For many years those were my thoughts. I wrote them in my journal daily. I saw those words when I looked in the mirror. They followed me throughout my day like a bubble in a comic strip. Then one day it hit me. Who am I trying to be somebody to? How can I be anything to anyone without being someone to myself <u>FIRST</u>?

I have been told every day, since the age of 6, that I am the reason someone else continues to breathe. Yet I still didn't feel worthy. For 24 years my sister, Terri Harper OB7637, has been incarcerated, only surviving the days by holding on to faith that she will come home to me. ME! <u>The "Nobody"</u>.

I was also able to experience love beyond the bars that confirmed I am somebody. Samantha Jo Dato placed me on a pedestal and allowed me to look in the mirror and see <u>Cashmere</u>. She has taught me self-care and the importance of living in my truth.

This book plays out my lost days and how I grew through and raised above them. It gives you an inside look into a unique way of thinking. It has been written to empower and uplift like-minded individuals.

I've included a 11 step *Soul Finding Plan*, complete with blank note pages to record your journey.

Follow these 11 easy steps to find the "somebody" in

yourself. Enjoy!

Thoughts of a Lost Soul

Lost Soul Rant #1

I wake up and drag myself to get my day started. The weight of the world is wearing on me. Gun shots, murders, jobs lost, abuse, mislead. I would have never thought I would live in a world without love. No compassion. I fear for myself. Question if I should reproduce. That would be child abuse in itself. And there is no one person to blame. Everyone plays a part in this cruel cold world. There is no way it can be changed by one person. Fighting back tears but I'm weak. Never thought I would be chosen to feel the hurt of the world. Now that I have this gift what am I suppose to do with it? If I share my feelings no one will understand. I may even be committed...

Hear my prayer

God, I see your vision. It's not as I sought it to be. Yet I will follow your path. There will be obstacles that are needed for me to reach the highest level of my strength. With that strength I will share my God-given gift with the world. I hope I become exactly who I am meant to be. I hope to make not only you, but also, myself proud. I have hit rock bottom so there's only room to go up. No one has ever seen this side of me. With this vulnerability, I will learn who Cashmere really is. The world will see who Cashmere has always been and finally get it.

Ramble

Blank page. Can't find the right words to fill it. No particular topic or issues to speak on. Exhausted with the same old lost soul, unwanted stories. So, where do I go from here, when nothing seems to change? My world is trapped inside a small box, which stays locked so no new, of any kind, can come in. I don't have a key or the number to a locksmith. 411 operators say that the call can't be connected. No escape. Still, I have more than half a page to go. Is it half full or half undone? And still my mind is a flat line. Music makes me dream. Takes me to a place I feel I should be. Put on that one song and its over. I'm here, in a place I shouldn't be. My outlook on life keeps me sane and thankful to make it to another day. What's my outlook? Everything happens because it is already planned; and I don't believe that my blueprint has all pain, so it will turn around.

If Only

If only I could give her all my love.

Show her that there is more to life than sorrow and pain.

If only I could give him all my joy.

Show him that there is more to life than abandonment and loss.

If only I could give them all my peace.

Show them that there is more to life than chaos and violence

If only I could change the world. Restore it to its original beauty.

Life was given to be united in harmony and rhythm.

If only we could unite.

Man's World

Good girl gone bad that what my folks say

But they never notice the good in me no way

So how can they tell if I'm good or bad,

 When they don't even see me?

When I lost Ms. Ellie I lost my whole family too

Opened up my eyes to see what's true

If it doesn't benefit them, they can give a fuck about what I go

through

Work so hard my toes bleed and my hands ache

No benefits, no sick days, no raises or 401ks

But my check is deducted if I take a half of hour break

Hell no! This shit ain't fair

But I guess I have to be a man for them to care

See they pacify him and slave me

I do the job twice as good but get paid half for the work

Because we live in a man's world.

Lost Soul Rant #2

Sometimes I wonder how things would be if Terri was never arrested, If my grandma had never left us so soon, if I were never born, if I didn't wake up this morning. Sometimes, thinking this way scares me, because God could one day show me. Don't get me wrong, I'm in no way questioning God because I am a true believer in everything happens as planned. Yet at the same time I believe that one's choices affect one's outcome. They kind of don't match, but that's what I believe. As I grow, I'm learning to make better choices and not getting overwhelmed when things don't go as planned.

Peace

Room with three windows

Two face a brick wall

The third lets in fresh air

Branches block the view

Yet, you still get a sense of

What's beyond them where the sun peeks through

Lyric

Taking all my pain and infusing it in my music

So when you bump it in your earphones my blood bleeds

through it

Keep taking shots when my hands are up

Guess I'm a threat to everybody when I stand up

Put everything into being a mother to your daughter

When her father wouldn't man up

Yet I'm left heartbroken like a woman who had a miscarriage

I must have a sign on my back that reads,

"Please keep stabbing"

But I will never stop loving

Love my enemies as I love my brother

When you love this hard you're bound to suffer

Been had a voice just removed the muzzle

It's the impact from the bite that leaves you puzzled

Infection in your steams like rabies

The best is yet to come Believe Me

Letter to Baby girl

This will be hard for you to understand. It's just as hard for me to have to write it. But I hope that one day you will believe like I do that I am making the best decision for both of us. The choice to let you go and no longer co- parent with your mother is one of the most difficult decisions I have ever and will ever make. Yet, to continue to drag us both through a winless battle would be unfair and unhealthy for you and I and our relationship.

I know it may be confusing for you. The promises and plans we made will no longer be possible. I know you were looking forward to me taking you on the Duck Ride and rock climbing for your birthday. I'm saddened that we will not be able to fulfill those adventures. I will miss out on you losing your first tooth and riding your bike without training wheels. I will miss us singing our good night song, making up silly dances on our way home from your school and picking out books at the bookstore.

I know you will have questions and need answers as to why I will no longer be your other mother or second mom. Your first mom may not want to tell you or give you the correct answers. So I will try my best to answer them now.

First I want you to know that in my heart you will always be my daughter and I will always be your other mom. I will not be in your everyday life anymore because your first mom and I are not friends anymore and we cannot agree on proper co-parenting. Because she is your first mom she has the last say in everything. If I was able to obtain my fair rights I would be able to fight for you until my last breath. Without those rights I am powerless to your first mom's laws. Which means at any given time she can and has taken you away from me.

No matter if I see you every day or never again, I want you to know that my love for you will never die. If you ever need me I will be there at the drop of a dime. I want you to remember what I taught you. Smile and laugh everyday. Be kind to others. Only kiss who you truly love. No one is perfect. You must accept the difference in people and yourself, for it's what makes you special. And the best rule of them all, families come in all different shapes. Having two moms makes you twice as blessed.

You are my most powerful inspiration. Since the first time you smiled at me, I have been motivated to be great. Just so I can show you greatness.

Love,

Mommy Cash

Better Choice

It's not me it's you.

I can never be option two.

I can't be option one if you have an option two.

It's not me it's you.

You want your cake and eat it too.

So, I've found someone who only wants to be my dessert.

Someone who treats me as I deserve

Like I'm the <u>ONLY OPTION</u>

Change Circles

I used to think my words weren't readable. I used to think my voice didn't matter. I thought what I stood for wasn't worth acknowledging. As I take on this journey of proving myself wrong, I realize that it was some of the people I was surrounded by that had me in that state of mind. The closer I get to the finish line, the fewer runners are by my side. I am okay with that. This is my dream. I can't expect you to chase it with me. Remember you are only as good as the 5 people you hang with. Choose your circle <u>wisely</u>.

Lost Soul Rant #3

What do you stand for?

Think about it for a second.

 If you do not stand for anything then you will lay with anything.

Loyalty cannot be your best quality.

Because when you are tested to choose from right or wrong,

loyalty is not an answer.

Loyalty cannot be how you measure things.

Is everything black and white?

Elevate

As I climb, the sun gets brighter to me.

As I climb, the shade gets darker for you.

You feel lost in my shadow.

You see my feet moving

 But you do not see my hand held out for yours.

This mountain is big enough for both of us.

Only hard work gets you to the top.

Are you willing to put in the sweat?

New Day

My grandmother's, the late Eleanor Bell, favorite song is *"What a Difference a Day Makes"* by Dinah Washington. Almost every day this past year I referred back to the words of that song. That song is about how love and the love from someone can change your whole outlook on life. How love can come when you are at your lowest and lead you back to cloud nine.

I started 2014, feeling unappreciated, mistreated, and with little hope of how I would make it through the year. I kept true to myself. I meditated and prayed. The answers came to me and I knew what I had to do. I had to go with love. Love has and will always be the answer. Yet, you have to know what love is. You also have to know that love doesn't always mean stay. To love someone or something means that you must know when to hold on and when to let go.

In with choosing love, I ended a 3-year relationship and rekindled a 29-year relationship with myself. In with choosing love, I lost a few friends but gained a handful of better ones. In with choosing love, I saw new places, learned new things and found my gift.

I am beginning 2015 with a promise and a plan. Both I will fulfill. Nothing or no one will get in my way. I have something to prove, and I intend to do just that. Allow me to introduce myself. I am **Cashmere Harper**. Now watch me be great.

Tears Of Frustration

When will you see me?

When will you remove yourself from the mirror?

And look at me?

Why is it so hard for you to bite the bullet?

And see that I am in need?

In need of your love and affection.

I give so much with nothing in return

My heart will soon dry out

Because you don't see me

You don't notice my tears

All you see is yourself

And your hurt

And your pain

And your past

You don't see me

I'm worried you never will.

Lost Soul Rant #4

Attachment is the root of all suffering. I know this. I believe this. I practice not to become attached to many things, people, or ideas. No matter how much I practice, there are some that I find myself attached to or some that are attached to me.

My Truth

Lesbianism is not my lifestyle. It's not my sexual preference. It's my culture, part of my identity, my background. I am a lesbian just like I am Black or an African American. See, I didn't just wake up one day and say I was a lesbian. I have been a lesbian from day one. This isn't a way of life this is my life. I was put on this earth to love women in the same way a man loves a woman.

I have studied gay and lesbian history the same way I have studied Black history. Being a lesbian woman doesn't make me any less of a woman. If anything, it makes me stronger. No matter who I love or am intimate with, it will not stop me from achieving the goals and dreams I have set for myself.

Being in a world where homosexuality is considered wrong makes it harder, yet it makes me even more determined to do more to make a difference. We allow "rules" and "regulations" from an era that no one, standing on this earth today, can tell you first hand how a power greater than all wanted us to live. We let fear separate us from peace and freedom.

And just to be clear, yes I am a lesbian and I am an author. But I am not a lesbian author. I am an author who just happens to me a lesbian.

Homeless

I just want to go home.

I have three sets of keys

Three different places to rest my head,

 But where is home?

I'm homeless with shelter

Who Matters?

#MikeBrown

I can sit and try to wrap my mind around this decision. Tell myself "maybe there was a piece of the puzzle that I didn't get." Just maybe there is some evidence that shows a different outcome of what I/we think happened. No matter how I try to look at it, at the end of the day no one deserves to have their life taken.

So what now?! Do I get my goons together and rally up and destroy other people or things that had nothing to do with it? NO!!! Now is the time to stand together. Encourage those to take a stand by not only showing that we are better than what they think of us but to uplift each other to do better than what they think of us. The only way to prevent this from happening again is to take care of our own. Become more involved in our communities. Clean up the streets ourselves. Show our youth that there is more to this life than the latest Jordan's or knowing how to do the "Na-Na".

We must read and learn and teach our history as well as our rights. Promote love and unity. Use this pain as a reminder of how hard the greats before us fought and now we must continue the fight.

My prayers are with Mike Brown, his family and each and every other person feeling the pain of having someone taken from them by violence.

#Baltimore

It amazes me how much negativity you people repost on social media. Yet have to be asked to share an encouraging friend's post... Where is the support? You complain how the world or generation is so lost but look at what you entertain. Look at what you send out into the world. If we support and share the good there could be far more to entertain. There could be less of what we see happening in Baltimore.

But what do I know? Who am I? Oh, just that friend that you have overlooked because I have something positive to share.

Where we messed up.

I think, as a people we got lost in the mindset of wanting to give our kids a "better life". Working so hard to give them better, we forgot to show them better. Moms working three jobs just so she can send her son to school with all the latest (shoes, clothes, phone, Beats by Dre, etc.). But she's not home enough to keep up with his schoolwork or make him dinner.

My generation is the generation of spoiled, lost brats. We don't know the value of a dollar. We don't know what it's like to truly work for anything. We've wasted so many years getting our way that now at 21- 25 years of age we don't know how to make our way.

I remember being the kid that didn't have the new Jordan's for Easter. Instead I had some bright orange champion sneakers. But I wore them proudly so when I got clown, I put myself out there as I was trendsetter. No one caught on but you couldn't knock my swag. I remember saying when I was old enough I would work hard to buy my own Jordan's. I remember when my baby girl was born I wanted to buy her all the Jordan's they had in her size. She was going to stay fly. She was going to have everything. I came home to show my mom all that I had bought.

She said, "child she can't even crawl yet." I said, "I know but I want her to have everything I didn't." She said, " What didn't you have?" I said " I cried for you to buy me Jordan's. Everybody on the block had them but me". She said, "everyone on the block went to public school but you didn't. I couldn't buy you Jordan's because I was paying for the fancy school you went to."

I had no come back. At that moment I took a long, hard look at my life and how I was raised. Up until that point I didn't know how truly blessed I was. No, I didn't have the new Jordan's, but I had attended some of the top schools in my city. No I didn't have Polo, but we ate dinner every night as a family. I couldn't stay out past the time the streetlights came on, because my mom sat and went over my schoolwork with me every school night. Now that I am able to count my blessings, I am able to bless others. I didn't take my baby girl's stuff back; however, I don't splurge on those things anymore. Instead, I opened up a trust fund for her future. I spoil her with my time and affection. I want to show her a better life. Show her that happiness is not measured by the amount of things you have. Happiness is measured by what you do with what you have.

Lost Soul Rant #5

How is it that it's so easy for you to speak your mind when you're fixing you're lips to nag and complain or say something negative, but you're speechless when it comes to giving thanks and love? You wish to destroy rather than to build.

#EricGarner

Ok, so let's take away the chokehold. Let's take away the resisting arrest. Let's just look at the part when they got him down and he was no longer moving. When his eyes rolled back and you no longer saw this 300-plus pound man was not breathing. What is the procedure when a life is fading in front of you? No one tried to give him CPR. He said he couldn't breathe. No one sat him up to get air. It took a while for the EMT to come and when they did I know they could tell he was no longer breathing. They didn't pull out oxygen or anything. That in my opinion is where it went wrong and every last one of those officers and EMT workers should be **FIRED AND CHARGED.**

No indictment

Text message from friend: "Cash, I feel some kind of way & I'm not sure that this is what I should feel. Everyone is outraged at the outcome of the Ferguson mess, but I already knew this would be the verdict. Because it's okay, to kill our brother & sisters. Not sure that I should even be upset because WE will forget about this in a few weeks. We're going to march with no cause, & raid & loot in our own communities. Because yea, that'll teach Whitey... "

My reply message: "I felt the same way at first. It's because you feel you personally can't change anything. You feel hopeless, and powerless. Individually we won't be able to scratch the surface. Yes, some will forget and go on as if it were nothing. But, if you don't forget you can keep it alive. I thought just as you did. I felt like why even post anything? Why even try? It's just me. Who is going to listen to little old me? You never know. Touching one person, getting one person to read and remember is critical, so when it dies down in the media we can keep it alive. As for the riots and looting there's not much you can do unless you are

present. You can continue to be the example of the right way to

do things."

We Matter

Black lives matter!!!

Black lives matter!!!

Hash tag

Hash tag

Our brown boys are being battered

By the boys in blue with badges and name tags

Hello Mrs. Officer

My name?

Cashmere Harper

And yes despite the uniqueness

That is the name my mother gave me

I know I have the right to remain silent but I prefer to use my

right to speak

See for so long I have lowered my head and tucked my tail

between my legs

For so long I have allowed things to happen

Turned the other cheek

And hope that my silence would show my pain

For so long I have thought to lead by example

But no one wants to follow a person with no voice

So let me be heard

The revolution will not be televised

And you won't be able to stream on your galaxy, iPhone or any

other mobile device

But it has been shot

Pun intended

It's been captured by a tiny lense attached to a bulletproof vest

and dash cam

Altered and republished

So that our tired minds think that there is nothing we can do

When the truth is we are breaking through.

Let me be heard

My young beautiful people of color

Stand up and be heard

We have a right to be here

And be safe

You have a right to live

Whichever way you choose to live

But no matter which way that is

Learn your history

Learn your rights

Soul Finding Plan

The New You

"In any field of endeavor, making a vow is the foundation for achieving

something great."

Make a vow to yourself. Think of things you have been putting

off. Think of what truly makes you happy and some of the things

that get in the way of your happiness. I vowed to live the life I am

supposed to live. Putting myself first, removing all the things and

people in my way.

Write your vows below and somewhere you can hang them up

and be encouraged daily. Read it out loud or

quietly to yourself whenever you find yourself lost or unsure of

where you want to go.

_____

_____

_____

_____

_____

_____

Fresh Start
"Start your day off with positive energy."

So many of us wake up, check social media, or turn on the news or have morning gossip with friends. We are inviting unwanted and unnecessary negative energy. I have removed social media and morning gossip phone calls from my morning routine. In fact. I don't take any phone calls, texts, or emails before 9am. I've added longer meditation sessions, prayer, yoga, and reading to my morning routine.

I encourage you to try it for a week. Instead of rolling over and grabbing your phone, wake up, say a prayer, and give thanks. Instead of turning on the news, get up and stretch for 10 minutes. Focus on your breathing. When you get to work, instead of jumping right into emails, Google motivational quotes. Do this for 7 days. Use the space below to make notes of how different your days have been.

_____

_____

Moving Forward
"Never touch anything with half your heart"

If your heart isn't into it, you will not do it any justice.   this is

true with anything: relationships, jobs, and projects. If someone

is not willing to give you their all, do not allow them so much

space in your world. That goes for lovers, friends, family, and

employers.

List some things you are doing that your heart is not in fully.

Then address them.

_____

_____

_____

_____

_____

_____

_____

_____

Making the list

Think of all the things/ people you love. List them below then
turn the page. **No cheating.**

_____

_____

_____

_____

_____

_____

_____

_____

_____

_____

_____

_____

_____

How long did it take you to list yourself???

If you are not in the top 3 of that list, it's time you start including

yourself. Take more time out for yourself. It is okay to love

yourself. In fact, no one can love you better. Use the space below

to jot down what you love about yourself. Fill in <u>all the lines,</u>

come back to this section as many times as you need to remind

yourself of your love for yourself .

_____

_____

_____

_____

_____

_____

_____

_____

_____

_____

Lesson Learned

"Nothing ever goes away until it teaches us

what we need to know"

Think of some things/situations that have you feeling like a

hamster on a wheel. What is it trying to teach you? Write down

some ways not to find yourself in the same things/situations.

Refer back to it when you find yourself in that same wheel again.

_____

_____

_____

_____

_____

_____

_____

_____

_____

Meditation

"You should sit in meditation for twenty minutes every day. Unless you're too busy; then you should sit for an hour." – Old Zen adage

People tend to over think meditation or put unrealistic expectations on meditation. Meditation is simply sitting still, with your thoughts, and focusing on your breathing or mantra*. By being still you are able to slow down your thoughts, push out ones that are causing negative energy, and find a sense of peace. I usually say a prayer at the end. I read that through meditation you can send vibrations into the universe that calls for peace in the world. So, how do you do it? Find a quiet place to sit. You just sit still for 20 or more minutes. With your eyes closed and inhale deep breaths with a small pause before you exhale. It's in those pauses that you will find peace. You can sit in a chair, on the floor or even stand. When I can't find a quiet space, I use headphones and play meditation music. Or I use the

*mantras

(originally in Hinduism and Buddhism) a word or sound repeated to aid concentration in meditation.

meditation made easy app. Sometimes I use prayer beads. But I encourage you to do research to find a way that fits you. Use the space below to list mantras*, or anything that will help with your meditation practice.

_____

_____

_____

_____

_____

_____

_____

_____

_____

_____

_____

_____

_____

---

*mantras

(originally in Hinduism and Buddhism) a word or sound repeated to aid concentration in meditation.

Stay Focused

"I know I am not where I want or should be, but I am closer than I

was yesterday"

If you are anything like me, by now, you have slipped back to your old ways, or have had to restart the process over a few times. That's ok! Reread your vow you wrote at the first step. If it no longer fits, make a new vow. Don't beat yourself up. You did not become lost overnight. And you won't find your way without trial and error. Use this space to write some encouraging words to yourself. Refer back to it the next time you loose your footing.

_____

_____

_____

_____

_____

_____

_____

Super Power

" Strengthen your power. No one is you and that is your power."

Name some things you can do better than anyone you know.

Today share some of those talents with the world.

_____

_____

_____

_____

_____

_____

_____

_____

_____

_____

_____

_____

_____

Stand Out

"If you don't fit in, then you are probably doing the right thing."

Today think of what separates you from the crowd and wear it with pride. God doesn't want you to be shy with his gift, but bold and loving and sensible. Show them who you are. Live in your truth. Below write about the new "You" that you have become.

_____

_____

_____

_____

_____

_____

_____

_____

_____

_____

_____

Continue the Journey

"By loving yourself first, you make it easier for others to love you."

Take care of yourself. The mind first, then the body and the soul will automatically fall into place. When these three are aligned, nothing will get in your way. When your practice is tested, do you give in and wash away all of your progress? Or do you stick to your guns? The results show just how far you have come. Keep in mind a true love story never ends. And you are your own love story...

_____

_____

_____

_____

_____

_____

_____

_____

About the Author

About the Author

*B*rilliant, *E*asy going, *S*trong and *T*alented comes to mind when

you think of the (B.E.S.T.) Author Cashmere Harper, with her

infectious smile, and love for family and friends. "Scooby", as she

is called by many loved ones is a powerful, self-discovered writer

who has continued to put thoughts onto paper effortlessly. She will indeed have your attention and draw you in with every line.

Born and Raised in Philadelphia Pennsylvania, she is now at a place in life where nothing can stop her. Having become an author in 2015 with her first book *"Thoughts of a Tainted Heart"* she is now in the process of opening her own publishing company Hope After 20 Publications (H/A20 Pub.).

H/A20 Pub. will provide authors of all ages and walks of life an atmosphere for their creativity and stories to be supported and uplifted, on a platform of victory, witnessed by all that turn the pages of their books. H/A20 Pub. will publish short stories, kid's books, autobiographies, cooking books, fictional, drama, action packed, non –traditional, judgment free, unrestricted styles of writing.

Cashmere found writing to be a great way to release feelings of brokenness and hurt at a very young age. With the death of her Grandma "YaYa" and the incarceration of her only sister and best friend Terri Harper, whom was sentenced to life in prison, she had no one to listen to her loss and hurt soul. So, she began to compose and convey her muddled feelings onto paper. Now at the tested age of 30 she has found so many people that have

been through or can relate to her life experiences. She is ready to

share her life lessons with the readers of today and the future.

Also By Cashmere

If you have been in a relationship, been in love, or brokenhearted; have a love or appreciation for poetry/literature this book is for you. ***"Thoughts Of A Tainted Heart"*** is the emotions of love and relationships expressed through poems and short stories. It's the first of the three part series "The Thought Process". It will capture you (the reader) with its moving words just as much as the bold cover art. Available on Amazon.com, Kindle, and IBooks.

Follow *Author Cashmere*

on social media:

Twitter: @AuthorCashmere

Facebook: www.facebook.com/AuthorCashmere

Instagram: @AuthorCashmere

Contact for booking and inquires:

author.cashmere@gmail.com

To order autograph copies:

http://www.mkt.com/cashmerebooks

Made in the USA
Middletown, DE
25 November 2015